Contents

Any words appearing in the text in bold, **like this**,
are explained in the Glossary.

Waterway habitats

Rivers and waterways are areas of moving freshwater, not salt water as found in seas and oceans. The rivers and waterways of the British Isles form a variety of very important **habitats** for many kinds of plants and animals.

Get this!

The Severn is the longest river in the British Isles at 342 kilometres long. The River Thames is so deep that ocean-going ships can travel up it to the Port of London!

What are rivers?

Rivers form naturally. They usually begin on mountains and hills. River water comes from rain or melted snow. The water flows downhill very quickly carving out rivers between banks of earth or rocks. At the **estuary**, or mouth of the river where it joins the sea, the water usually flows slowest because the land is flatter.

Other waterways

Many waterways in the British Isles, such as canals, are **artificial** rivers. Canals get their constant supply of water from rivers and streams, but people built them. Other channels may have been dug to create waterways between rivers and lakes, or to carry **irrigation** water.

Viewed from the air, this British river looks rather like a snake as it twists between fields. ➔

WILD HABITATS
of the British Isles

Rivers and Waterways

Louise and Richard Spilsbury

Heinemann
LIBRARY

www.heinemann.co.uk/library
Visit our website to find out more information about **Heinemann Library** books.

To order:
☎ Phone 44 (0) 1865 888066
🖹 Send a fax to 44 (0) 1865 314091
💻 Visit the Heinemann Bookshop at www.heinemann.co.uk/library to browse our catalogue and order online.

First published in Great Britain by Heinemann Library, Halley Court, Jordan Hill, Oxford OX2 8EJ, part of Harcourt Education.

Heinemann is a registered trademark of Harcourt Education Ltd.

Editorial: Lucy Thunder and Helen Cannons
Design: David Poole and Kamae Design
Picture Research: Hannah Taylor and Liz Savery
Production: Edward Moore

Originated by P.T. Repro Multi-Warna
Printed in China by WKT Company Limited

The paper used to print this book comes from sustainable resources.

ISBN 0 431 12121 4 (hardback)
08 07 06 05 04
10 9 8 7 6 5 4 3 2 1

ISBN 0 431 12128 1 (paperback)
09 08 07 06 05
10 9 8 7 6 5 4 3 2 1

British Library Cataloguing in Publication Data

Spilsbury, Louise and Spilsbury, Richard
Rivers and Waterways. – (Wild habitats of the British Isles)
577.6'4'0941
A full catalogue record for this book is available from the British Library.

Acknowledgements
The Publishers would like to thank the following for permission to reproduce photographs: FLPA/B Borrell Casals p**10**; FLPA/Celtic Photo Library p**4**; Heather Angel/Natural Visions p**8**; Mark Boulton p**7**; Nature Picture Library/Dietmar Nill p**20**; NHPA/Alan Barnes p**13**; NHPA/C Guy & P Enjelvin p**14**; NHPA/David Woodfall pp**9, 28, 29**; NHPA/G I Bernard p**17**; NHPA/Laurie Campbell p**6**; NHPA/Stephen Dalton p**11**; NHPA/Stephen Krasemann p**23**; Ordnance Survey pp**12** top, **16** top, **22** top; Oxford Scientific Films p**19**; Oxford Scientifc Films/Rodger Jackman p**22** bottom; Oxford Scientific Films/Ben Osborne p**26**; Oxford Scientific Films/Colin Milkins pp**15, 27**; Woodfall Wild Images/Andy Harmer p**18**; Woodfall Wild Images/David Woodfall pp**12** bottom, **24**; Woodfall Wild Images/J Macpherson p**16** bottom; Woodfall Wild Images/Mark Hamblin p**21**.

Cover photograph of a fast-flowing stream, reproduced with permission of National Trust Photographic Library/Joe Cornish.

The Publishers would like to thank Michael Scott, wildlife consultant and writer, for his assistance in the preparation of this book.

Every effort has been made to contact copyright holders of any material reproduced in this book. Any omissions will be rectified in subsequent printings if notice is given to the Publishers.

Disclaimer

River and waterway habitats

A habitat is a place where different organisms (living things) live. Rivers can contain several different kinds of habitats. Some parts of a river are fast flowing, while others move slowly. Some riverbeds are rocky; others may be sandy or muddy. The sides or banks of a river or waterway form different habitats depending on whether they are rocky, grassy or sandy. The animals and plants that live in these different habitats are **adapted** to live there – they are ideally suited to the special conditions their particular habitat provides.

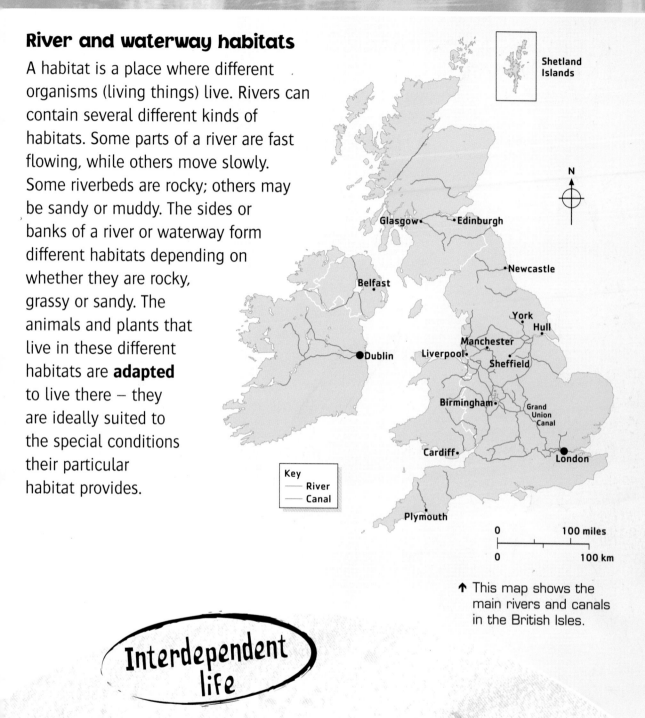

Shetland Islands

N

Glasgow·   ·Edinburgh

·Newcastle

Belfast

York
Hull·
Manchester·
Liverpool·   ·Sheffield
●Dublin

Birmingham·   Grand Union Canal

Cardiff·
London●

Plymouth

Key	
——	River
——	Canal

0   100 miles
0   100 km

↑ This map shows the main rivers and canals in the British Isles.

Interdependent life

The lives of the plants and animals in a river or waterway are closely connected. They rely on each other for survival. For example, kingfishers are birds that do not eat plants, but they eat fish such as minnows, which do eat plants. If there are not enough plants in a river, there will be fewer minnows for kingfishers to eat. This reliance on each other is called interdependency.

Forming waterways

Most rivers in the British Isles formed a long time ago. When rain falls and snow melts on mountains and hills, most of the water flows down the slopes. As water flows downhill it gains speed and force.

A river's journey

In the past when water rushed down mountains and hills, it washed away stones and mud and wore bits from the rocks. These bits of stone and rock eroded the land as water passed over it, carving out channels in the land that became rivers and streams. The upper stretches of a river, where the water is moving fastest and strongest, are often straighter, because the water has had more power to cut itself a straight course.

↑ It is difficult for many plants and animals to live in a river **habitat** like this because the water is usually moving so quickly.

Fast-swimming trout

Trout have strong muscles compared to many similar sized fish and can swim swiftly. This allows them to survive even in the faster-flowing upper reaches of rivers, such as the Thames. If you catch a glimpse of a shiny fish with dappled spots on its back, in a river, it might be a trout.

When the river is lower down, in its middle stretches, its water is not moving so quickly. Rather than carving a path through obstacles such as areas of harder rock, the river tends to form around them. These winding bends in rivers are called meanders and can be quite deep. As a river nears the sea it usually becomes wider and slower. As the river runs out of **energy** it deposits (drops) the mud it is carrying. That is why the lower stretches of a river usually have sandy or muddy bottoms.

How were canals formed?

Canals were built in Britain in the 18th century at a time when water transport was very important. Many industrial areas, especially in the north, simply did not have suitable rivers to transport their goods. Canals – **artificial** rivers – were dug to connect important places together, and to link certain areas to rivers or the sea. Canals are usually fairly deep all the way along and they flow quite slowly.

Get this!

The water in rivers and waterways never runs out because it is constantly being replaced. This process is called the water cycle. Water from the Earth **evaporates** into clouds, cools down and returns to Earth again as rain and snow!

← Most canals usually have concrete or brick sides in which wildlife cannot live. However, the banks and grass alongside canals have become popular pathways for wildlife.

River and waterway plants

Although few plants can grow on the bed of a fast-flowing river, or in very deep water, many grow along the banks of rivers and waterways. Plants also grow in the water of slower-moving rivers, both at the river's edge and in shallow riverbeds.

Growing from the riverbed

Some water plants grow with their roots anchored in shallow riverbeds. These plants have long stems that float in the water. The stems hold up leaves to catch the light they need to make food in **photosynthesis**.

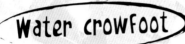

If you see a water plant with two kinds of leaves it could be water crowfoot. This water plant has some flat leaves that float on the water's surface to catch light. It also has different, feathery leaves below water that are not damaged when water flows around and through them.

Floating plants

In slow-moving rivers and canals, some plants float on the water's surface. Most have roots that trail in the water, to absorb the water and extra **nutrients** that plants need. Duckweed is a tiny floating plant that quickly spreads over wide areas. **Algae** are tiny plants that float in the water like a green soup.

Floating bur-reed has long thin leaves that float easily with the flow of the **current** to reach the light near the water's surface. ➔

Life on the edge

Mosses, ferns and other plants that thrive in damp, shady conditions grow on the banks of rivers and waterways. Many plants, such as reeds and watercress, grow in the shallow water at the edge of slow-moving rivers and streams, with just their roots under water.

River and waterway trees

Some trees grow particularly well with their roots in damp soils. These include willow and beech trees. Seeds from these trees often grow in cases designed to float. When they fall into the water they can wash onto ground further downstream and may **germinate**.

Life-giving plants

Plants living in the water are a vital part of river and waterway **habitats**. When they make their own food using the process of photosynthesis, they release oxygen into the water. Animals need this **oxygen** to live. Plants also provide important cover for many animals to shelter and **breed** in.

← The trees that grow along the edge of rivers hold the soil together and help stop the bank being **eroded** by the moving water.

River mini-beasts

Rivers and waterways and their banks are ideal **habitats** for many **invertebrates** and small animals. They can shelter among plants or between riverbed stones out of reach of the **current**. Some live their whole lives in water; others hatch from eggs under water and then emerge and live on land as adults. Many, including water snails, feed on the plants or on the dead plant life and animal material that washes into the water and rots. Others feed on the **larvae** of **insects**, or on each other!

The larvae of such insects as mayflies, caddis flies and dragonflies, grow into adults under the water. They have **gills** so they can breathe. After they turn into adults, they breathe air and fly over rivers and canals to catch tiny insects to eat.

Get this!

Water boatmen are insects that get their name from their oar-shaped legs! When they paddle underwater, they take a bubble of air with them, rather like a scuba diver, so they can breathe.

↑ Mayfly larvae feed on algae on riverbed rocks. They have a flat body and cling to rocks to avoid getting washed away by the current.

When caddis fly larvae
hatch out of their eggs
they build cases for themselves
out of tiny stones and bits of plants. They stay
inside these cases for safety and poke out their
heads to feed. When they have grown fully, they
leave the cases and fly out of the river. They live for
just a few days, long enough to **breed** and lay eggs
of their own.

Caddis fly larvae

River animals with shells

Some river animals are protected by shells. River snails
have a single shell shaped like a spiral, which can be
up to 5 centimetres long. They eat **algae** from the
surface of underwater stones using a rough tongue.
Other **molluscs**, like mussels, have two shells. The
swan mussel, which buries itself in gravel riverbeds,
is the commonest of these.

Dragonfly larvae, which
live in water, eat almost
anything smaller than
themselves. As adults, like
this one, dragonflies eat
other flying insects, such
as mosquitoes, midges,
butterflies and moths.

Norfolk Broads, England

The Norfolk Broads is a large area of human-made lakes that extend over the slow-moving parts of five rivers. Dips in the land were created by people digging up land for **peat** from the 12th to the 14th centuries. The dips then flooded when the sea level rose, forming broads. Rivers and **artificial** channels connecting the broads form inland waterways that are home to many plants and animals.

↑ This map shows the area known as Hickling Broad, part of the Norfolk Broads in East Anglia.

Plants of the Broads

The most common plant of the Broads is the reed, a kind of grass that lives only in damp soils. Reeds can grow up to 3 metres tall. They have tough stems and grow closely together to form dense beds. Colourful wildflowers that thrive in damp soils also live among the reedbeds. These include marsh sowthistle, with its dandelion-like flowers that show above the reeds, and purple loosestrife, which has bright purple spikes of flowers.

↑ The edges of the Norfolk Broads are cloaked in thick reeds where many birds and insects make their homes.

Butterflies and moths

The reeds and other plants among the waterways of the Broads provide food and shelter to many butterflies and moths. These include some unusual **species** such as the brown reed leopard moth, which has a wingspan of between 2.5 and 5 centimetres, and the creamy yellow and black swallowtail butterfly, with a wingspan of about 8 centimetres. The main difference between butterflies and moths is that moths fly by night, whereas butterflies are active in the day. Also, moths have hairy **antennae** to pick up scent, while butterflies have slender antennae. Many butterflies and moths lay their eggs on particular kinds of plants, so that when the **larvae** hatch out of the eggs they can feed on the plant's leaves.

Get this!

The Norfolk Broads is home to over 250 different species of flowering plants, many of which cannot be found anywhere else in Britain.

The swallowtail butterfly

The swallowtail is Britain's largest and most exotic looking butterfly. Sadly this beautiful butterfly is quite rare and only found in parts of East Anglia, such as the Norfolk Broads. The problem is that the swallowtail larvae eat only one kind of food plant – milk parsley – and milk parsley only thrives in damp soils. As wet areas of land are drained and taken over for farming or building, milk parsley plants die out and so does the swallowtail.

13

Fish of the waterways

Fish hatch from eggs laid underwater and spend their whole lives in water. Fish bodies are perfectly **adapted** for underwater life. They breathe underwater using special body parts called **gills**. They swim by moving their bodies from side to side and their smooth, **streamlined** body shape helps them to move through flowing water. They have **fins** for braking and for keeping them upright and steady. Different kinds of fish live in different kinds of rivers. Trout usually live alone in cool, clear, fast-moving rivers. Perch usually live in groups called shoals and prefer canals and slow-moving rivers.

Fish food

Some fish in streams, rivers and canals eat plants. Others eat small animals that feed on those plants, such as snails, or **insects** and other fish. Fish have different ways of catching food. The brown trout stays in one place and waits for food such as insect **larvae** and drowned flies to be washed into its mouth. Barbel and bream suck in worms, snails and larvae from the riverbed.

Barbel fish

The barbel gets its name from its whisker-like barbels (feelers). These are covered with taste buds. They are used to feel and taste for food as the barbel swims along the bottom of murky, slow-flowing rivers.

Residents and visitors

Some of the fish in Britain's rivers are residents – they live there all the time – while others are only visiting. Young brown trout and sea trout both hatch from eggs laid in gravel riverbeds. Brown trout then remain in freshwater all their lives, while the silvery sea trout **migrate** to the sea to feed and grow into adults, then return to rivers to **breed**.

↑ Pike are the hunters of the river. They find **prey** by smelling them or sensing their movements and catch them using rows of sharp, backward-pointing teeth. Pike eat almost anything they can catch, including fish, ducklings and frogs. This pike is eating a newt.

Get this!

Many river fish have the top part of their body darker than their belly. This protects them from **predators**. When a predator looks up from below, the fish's pale belly cannot easily be seen against the light sky above. From above, its dark back makes it hard to spot against the darker water below!

River Spey, Scotland

The River Spey is the second-longest river in Scotland. A huge mass of ice slid across the land 2.5 million years ago and carved out the valley through which the river runs today. The River Spey flows from the Grampian Mountains to the sea.

Rare animals

Many animals live in the clear waters and riverbed of the River Spey. These include three especially rare **species**: freshwater pearl mussels, sea lampreys and Atlantic salmon. Freshwater pearl mussels can grow up to 15 centimetres long and they have dark brown shells. They feed by extracting tiny bits of plant or animal matter from the water as they suck water through their shells. These **molluscs** have become rare, mainly because they need to live in the gravel or sand of clean waterways, such as the River Spey, and many rivers are now **polluted**.

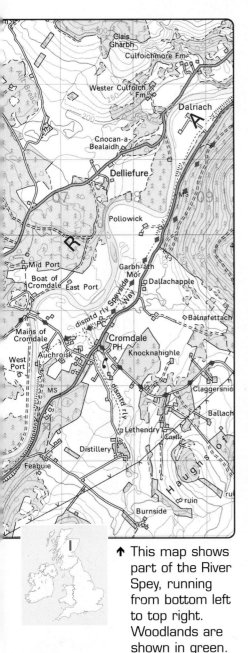

↑ This map shows part of the River Spey, running from bottom left to top right. Woodlands are shown in green.

↑ One reason pearl mussels are rare is that people still collect them to take the valuable pearls that grow inside them, even though it is against the law to do so.

Fish of the Spey

There are many different fish in the River Spey, including brown trout and sea trout, pike, minnows and eels. The sea lamprey is one of the most unusual. The eel-like adults are grey-brown and grow up to 90 centimetres long. They spend their first five to eight years feeding on rotting plant matter in the riverbed. Then they **migrate** to the sea and clamp their funnel-shaped mouth on to a larger fish, such as cod or haddock. They feed by scraping off flesh with their rough tongue and sucking out blood from the larger fish, and eventually kill it.

Get this!

Freshwater pearl mussels can live for up to 100 years. They are amongst the longest lived of all invertebrates.

Atlantic salmon

If you see a fish leaping out of the water, it is likely to be a salmon. Atlantic salmon return to the River Spey from the sea to **breed** every autumn. They swim upstream, against the **current**, and often leap up waterfalls. They return to the river in which they were born to lay their eggs in the gravel riverbed. After three years, the young salmon that hatch from those eggs follow the river downstream and to sea. This picture shows a baby salmon hatching from one egg.

River and waterway birds

Many different kinds of birds live and have their young around rivers or visit waterways to feed. Most river and waterway birds feed on the plants or animals that live among the water.

Kingfisher parents catch small fish such as minnows as food for their chicks. The chicks need about fifteen fish per day! ↓

Feeding in rivers

Some birds prefer slow-moving rivers and canals. The moorhen looks black and has a red and yellow beak. It feeds mainly on plants at the edge of the river. Coots are black all over except for a white beak. They usually dive to get water plants to eat, up to 7 metres below the surface. The female mallard duck is mottled brown and the male has a striking green head. Mallards feed by dipping their heads underwater to reach plants and small waterway animals.

Kingfishers swoop down quickly from a perch above the river to catch fish, **insects** or snails in their sharp beaks.

Other birds live by fast-moving parts of a river. For example, the grey wagtail, a small bird with a grey back and yellow belly, flies over the surface of fast-moving water picking off mayflies, mosquitoes and midges.

Nesting by waterways

Many birds nest among the tall reeds and grasses at the edge of a waterway, in the trees by the banks, or on bridges and canal-side buildings. These all make good nest sites because they provide shelter from bad weather and **predators**. They are also close to the water, so the birds can collect food. Kingfishers nest in chambers hollowed out of sandy banks. Mallards generally nest on the ground. Moorhens make large nests out of dead reeds and twigs lined with grasses, among clumps of plants in the water.

Dippers

Dippers are river birds that can 'walk' and swim underwater, using their wings as oars and their strong claws to grip stones. Dippers can stay underwater for about 30 seconds to catch caddis fly, stonefly and mayfly **larvae**. You might see one perched on a boulder in a fast-flowing river, nervously dipping its white-chested body up and down.

Waterway mammals

Many **mammals** visit rivers to drink, but several different kinds live near water all the time. They swim and find food in rivers and waterways. The banks of rivers and canals are usually also fairly quiet and leafy places, so mammals can travel between different parts of the waterway safely.

Water voles

Water voles, like many other waterway mammals, have sleek, thick, oily coats of hair. Water runs off this kind of coat instead of soaking into the animal's skin, so the animal does not get too wet and cold. Water voles are sometimes mistaken for brown rats, which also swim. Unlike brown rats, water voles have reddish-brown hair, very small rounded ears and a furry tail. They paddle or dive using all four limbs to move along. Water voles mainly live along the leafy banks of slow-moving rivers and eat grasses and other plants. They dig burrows in the riverbank with different rooms for sleeping and nesting.

Bats are the only flying mammals in the British Isles. Daubenton's bats, like this one, usually live in woodland near a river. At night they fly over water, scooping up **insects** to eat using their tail and feet. ↓

Water shrews

At around 7 centimetres long, water shrews are the biggest of the shrews in the British Isles. They have a long pointed snout, small ears and tiny eyes. Water shrews live in burrows near rivers and streams. They dive and swim to catch freshwater shrimps, small fish and caddis fly **larvae**. They use their bristly feet as paddles.

One of the wildlife signs to look out for by rivers are otter droppings, like the ones shown, which often contain fish bones. Otters use droppings to mark their territory – to tell their neighbours which area belongs to them. Otters use the claws on their feet to catch and hold down food, mainly slippery fish, but also small mammals, birds and frogs. They usually hunt at night and rest in a hole in the riverbank during the day. Otters have webbed feet (skin between their toes) which they use like oars to swim far and fast.

Otter cubs (young) are born in holes among riverbank tree roots or under rocks. Like all mammals, their first food is their mother's milk. Then the mother catches fish for them. Otter cubs take their first swim at about ten weeks old.

The River Severn begins in mid-Wales and flows 340 kilometres before joining the sea at the Bristol Channel. The water in the Severn is fast-flowing for most of its length, until it reaches the large **estuary** where the water rises and lowers with the **tides**. The Severn is an important river for several kinds of **migratory** fish, including salmon, eels and sea lamprey, as well as resident fish such as brown trout, barbel, perch and pike.

A home for mammals

Along the length of the Severn, there are several different kinds of **habitat**, from mudflats and sandbanks to shingle and rocky shores. These provide homes for different **mammals** such as water voles, brown rats and mink, many of which feed on its rich stock of fish.

↑ This map shows part of the River Severn. The red diamond shapes mark out a nature trail that runs along the river.

Eels in the Severn

Young eels – called elvers – arrive in the River Severn after a journey of around 6400 kilometres (4000 miles), lasting three years. They come all the way from where they hatch in the Sargasso Sea, which surrounds the Bahamas in the Caribbean. They stay in the Severn for between eight and fifteen years. Young eels feed at night on small animals and rest during the day buried in mud at the riverbed. When they are fully grown they swim downstream and return to the sea to swim all the way back to the Sargasso to **breed**!

Brown rats

Brown rats live all over the British Isles. They are strong swimmers and are also found along many canals and waterways, including the River Severn. Brown rats are very successful and increase in number so quickly because they eat almost anything. Adult females can also have up to fifteen young in a litter and five litters a year! They find their way around in the dark using their sense of touch and by feeling the way with their sensitive whiskers.

The story of mink

The mink is a mammal the size of a small cat, with very dark brown fur. The wild mink that live in the British Isles were originally brought from America to be farmed for their fur. They escaped from fur farms in the 1930s and began to breed in the wild. Around the River Severn, wild mink eat fish, birds and small mammals, such as water voles.

Get this!

The River Severn has the second highest tidal range (the difference between high and low tide) of any river in the world!

Wild mink like this one are fierce hunters killing not only wild **prey**, but also small farm animals. ➜

Changes through the year

The different temperatures and number of hours of daylight that come with the different seasons – spring, summer, autumn and winter – are responsible for many of the changes that occur in rivers and waterways throughout the year.

In summer, waterways are at their busiest. Flowers are in full bloom and young fish, waterbirds and mammals that have recently been born are eating as much as they can to build up strength for the coming winter. ↓

Spring and summer

As winter turns to spring and then summer, the days get longer. There are more hours of light and the weather gets warmer. Sunlight is the main source of **energy** for plants. The increased amount of light in spring and summer triggers plants to grow and produce flowers. As plant activity increases, so does animal life. **Insects**, moths and butterflies eat flower **nectar** and gain the energy they need to produce eggs. Birds, such as swifts and swallows, come to hunt the insects. Most animals – including waterbirds, fish and **mammals**, such as otters – have their young in spring and summer. This is because there is more food about and the water is warmer and not as rough as it can be in autumn and winter.

Autumn and winter

In autumn and winter the days become shorter, colder and damper. In autumn, seeds from riverside plants such as the alder tree fall into the water. They wash ashore further downstream and rest until spring when they begin to grow. Most plants drop their leaves and stop growing during winter.

There are fewer animals around in winter. As food supplies get scarcer many insects die. Some fish swim into warmer, deeper waters until spring. Others lie still to save energy and only feed every few days. Many waterway birds, such as swallows, **migrate** to warmer countries for winter. River mammals, such as the water shrew, have thick fur so they can swim and hunt all year round.

Mayflies emerge from waterways in late spring. **Larvae** live for several years underwater before they become adults. They survive cold winters by burrowing into the silt of the riverbed. When they leave the water as adults, they **breed** and die the same day!

← Plants trap the Sun's energy to make food. Animals get energy by eating plants or other animals that eat plants. A **food web** is a series of living things that eat each other. This is a diagram of a river food web in summer.

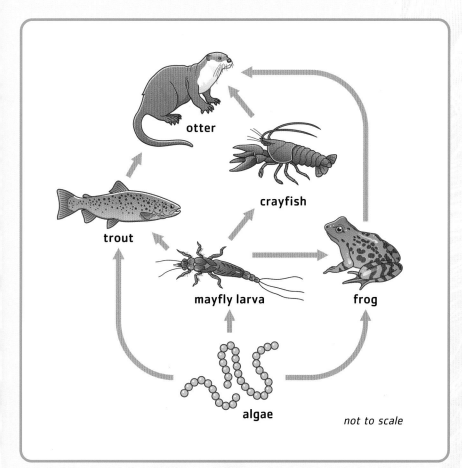

otter

crayfish

trout

mayfly larva

frog

algae

not to scale

Under threat

Most freshwater wildlife thrives in clean, clear water. The biggest threat to rivers and waterways in the British Isles is **pollution**. Pollution comes in many forms. Some pollution is caused by rainwater mixing with pollution in the air to form **acid rain**. This then falls or drains into waterways. Some industries, built along rivers, also illegally pour waste chemicals into the water. Acid rain and such chemicals can be poisonous to small water animals and fish.

Dangers

Sometimes farm slurry (liquid manure) or other farm pollutants such as **fertilizers** runs into rivers and waterways. Chemicals called nitrates in these pollutants encourage **algae** to grow. When algae die, the **bacteria** that decompose (rot) them use up a lot of **oxygen**. This reduces the amount of oxygen left in the water for other living things to use. Litter is another form of pollution. It can clog rivers and make the water dirty. Discarded tins and bottles can even trap and kill small water animals, including fish.

Water pollution can be disastrous for river life. For example, if water pollution kills off many **insects** it can affect populations of birds, such as dippers, which feed on them. ↓

Riverside activities

Sometimes plants from river and canal banks are cleared or cut back. This robs animals such as water voles of plant foods and otters of plant cover that they use for shelter. When dredging machines are used to clean river bottoms of mud or litter this also disturbs and frightens river wildlife. It can stop birds from nesting and is known to prevent otters from **breeding**.

Breaking the links in a food web

The plants and animals in rivers and waterways are dependent upon the river and upon each other for food and shelter. Humans have done a lot of damage by interfering with this delicate balance. In and around many rivers, plants brought from other countries have spread and taken over from **native** plants. This reduces the number of food plants available to some native animal **species**. In some rivers, the **predator** mink, originally from North America, has wiped out entire populations of native water voles.

white-clawed crayfish

The number of native white-clawed crayfish (shown here) is reducing due to American signal crayfish. These were first brought to Britain for fish farming in ponds. They escaped and began **breeding** in the wild. Signal crayfish spread a disease that can kill white-clawed crayfish.

Protecting waterways

Rivers and waterways need protection because they are very important wildlife **habitats**. They also supply us with clean water and are beautiful wild places that give us pleasure when we visit or walk along them.

How do people care for rivers and waterways?

There are laws to stop people dumping waste in rivers and waterways. The government also controls any changes to stretches of river, such as new buildings. The Environment Agency has been given powers by the government to check rivers and waterways in England and Wales to see how **polluted** they are. Anyone breaking the law can be fined or taken to court. You can report any river pollution you see to the National Rivers Authority. There are also several **conservation** organizations, such as Worldwide Fund for Nature (WWF) and Friends of the Earth, which work to protect rivers and waterways.

Canal conservation

In the last ten years, there has been a great deal of interest in restoring canals. British Waterways has restored many stretches of canals. In Scotland, for example, the old canals that linked the cities of Edinburgh and Glasgow have been restored and reopened.

← These children are getting involved in clearing rubbish that has been polluting a river in Manchester.

What you can do

Homes in the British Isles use much more water today than they did in the past. On average each of us uses over 150 litres a day, for drinking, washing, cooking and so on. Water companies take water from reservoirs or under the ground. They also take water from rivers and this can affect wildlife. You can help by reducing the amount of water you use. Try taking showers instead of baths, turn the tap off when brushing your teeth and make sure taps are turned off properly.

Get this!

Even though the world is covered in so much water, only about 1 per cent of it is fresh water that we can use: the rest is salt water.

↑ National RiverWATCH is a project that involves schoolchildren in studying the quality of the freshwater in rivers and waterways. This helps wildlife trusts find out if a waterway is being polluted or damaged.

Otter success story

In the 1950s and 1960s otters disappeared from many British rivers due to water pollution. In recent years, water companies have cleaned up rivers and even helped otters by building dens for them to live in. Now otters are returning to rivers.

Glossary

acid rain rainwater that has been polluted by chemicals in the air, making it acidic and damaging to wildlife

adapted when a living thing has special features that help it to survive in its particular habitat

algae plants that can make their own food by photosynthesis, but which do not have leaves, stems or roots

antennae pair of feelers on an insect's head used to feel or taste

artificial made by people; not natural

bacteria microscopic organisations that are found in the soil, water and air

breed to have young and increase in number

conservation taking action to protect plants, animals and wild habitats

current moving water stream in a river or sea

energy all living things need energy in order to live

erode when land is worn away

estuary part of river where it widens and meets the sea

evaporate when water turns from a liquid to a gas

fertilizers sprays or powders that farmers use to help plants grow bigger

fin strong flap of skin on a fish that it uses for swimming and steering

food web diagram that shows the order in which food energy is passed from plants to animals

germinate when a plant sprouts from a seed and begins to grow shoots and roots

gills special body parts that allow an animal to breathe underwater

habitat natural place where groups of plants and animals live

insect small six-legged animals which, when adult, have bodies divided into three sections: head, thorax (chest) and abdomen (stomach)

invertebrate animal without a backbone

irrigation watering of land by farmers so that they can grow crops

larvae young stage in life cycle of some animals between hatching from an egg and becoming an adult

mammals type of animal with some hair on their bodies. Female mammals can give birth to live young which they feed on their own milk.

migrate/migratory when animals regularly move from one place to another and back again

molluscs group of animals that includes snails, mussels, slugs, octopuses and squids

native living naturally in a particular place

nectar sugary substance plants make to attract animals which like to eat it

nutrients kinds of chemicals that nourish plants and animals

oxygen gas in the air that animals breathe in and which living things need to survive

peat partly rotted remains of moss plants

photosynthesis process by which plants make their own food using water, carbon dioxide and energy from sunlight

pollute/pollution when chemicals or waste escape into the air, water or soil and damages the habitat there for plants and animals

predator animal that catches and eats other animals

prey animal that is caught and eaten by another animal

species group of living things that are similar in many ways and can breed together

streamlined shape rather like a torpedo, which allows water or air to flow around it easily

tides rise and fall of the sea. At high tide the sea rises up the shore. At low tide it flows away from it.

Find out more

Books

Discover Nature in Water and Wetlands: Things to Know and Things to Do, E. Lawlor and P. Archer (Stackpole Books, 2000)

Great Rivers of Britain and Ireland (Great Rivers), Michael Pollard (Evans Brothers, 2002)

Pocket Guide to Freshwater Fishes of Britain, Alwyne Wheeler (Collins and Brown, 1999)

Websites

The following organizations work to look after rivers and canals in the British Isles:
www.thewaterwaystrust.co.uk (The Waterways Trust)
www.wildlifewatch.org.uk (National RiverWATCH)
www.wildlifetrusts.org (the junior branch of The Wildlife Trusts)
www.btcv.org (British Trust for Conservation Volunteers)
www.environment-agency.gov.uk (The Environment Agency has a kids' section with games, information on water and what the agency is doing to protect waterways in Britain. There are also movies to show you how our lives affect the environment.)

National Rivers Authority have a telephone helpline where you can report any river pollution you spot: 0800 807 060
The Worldwide Fund for Nature (WWF) works to protect threatened rivers and river wildlife around the world: www.panda.org

Index